Purple Lucid Dreams

Remya Ramakrishnan

Ukiyoto Publishing

All global publishing rights are held by

Ukiyoto Publishing

Published in 2024

Content Copyright © Remya Ramakrishnan

ISBN 9789361720055

All rights reserved.
No part of this publication may be reproduced,
transmitted, or stored in a retrieval system, in any form
by any means, electronic, mechanical, photocopying,
recording or otherwise, without the prior permission of
the publisher.

The moral rights of the authors have been asserted.

This is a work of fiction. Names, characters, businesses,
places, events, locales, and incidents are either the
products of the author's imagination or used in a fictitious
manner. Any resemblance to actual persons, living or
dead, or actual events is purely coincidental.

This book is sold subject to the condition that it shall not by
way of trade or otherwise, be lent, resold, hired out or
otherwise circulated, without the publisher's prior
consent, in any form of binding or cover other than that in
which it is published.

www.ukiyoto.com

Dedication

I dedicate this book to my mother, Rethy Ramakrishnan for her consistent prayers that keep me safe. I believe it's her prayers that have kept me alive amidst all this chaos.Amma, 'I will be your never-growing-up child'. I'm grateful to my blood and brother, Rejeesh Vathiyath, who breathes my dreams. I owe him for everything I'm today. My heartfelt acknowledgment to my father, Ramakrishnan Vathiyath. Thank you, I write because I inherit his purple innocence and crowded head.I'm also grateful to my research guide, Dr. Rukmini S for her constant support and kindness. Most importantly my best friend, Hima Raju, thank you for understanding the language of my heart. and not giving up on me whenever I gave up on myself.

Contents

I'm not My Hair	1
Blue	3
Ravi Chettan	5
Lucid Dreams	7
Behind Your Name	10
Flowers of Sunsets	13
Baptize Empty Tears.	15
Mermaids	18
Home	19
Funeral	20
Palace Of Lies	22
Final Calling	24
Claustrophobic Memories	25
Fishing Death	26
Cobwebs	28
Blue Moon	30
Capsuled Poems	32
Egg Toast	34
About the Author	35

I'm not My Hair

I tell them I'm not my hair.
I read Woolf and cry with her poems.
I fall for men who can't be my poems.

At night, I take all my emotions in a purple jar,
paint them blue,
and tell the world,
blue is my color.

I live purple when they think I'm blue.
I sell my truth in white lies
and dying guilt,
guilt I borrowed
from all who sold me for a moment's Cloud 9.

I have broken bangles and a yellow flower for my heart.
I cry. I panic. I run to the therapist
who cries in the middle of the night
when all his patients are sleeping.

I sit with him and read my poems.
He wants to run.
I want to crawl back to my mother's womb
and beg her not to give birth to me again.

Let me sleep there all my life.
Sing me Pan's Labyrinth lullaby.
"I don't want to come out and look at people
who don't look like me and know I'm the monster".
And bang my head against wall
every time I leave my body in search of a soul.

Blue

I hear a nightingale singing
when you hold Blue close to show the cat
hiding behind the white curtain.
My wildness abandons me to take a stroll
 in the wilderness where I buried
 your flowers waiting for your return.
Stay with me and sing us our favourite lullaby.
Come, let's sleep on the green grass all this winter.
Let's wake up only in Autumn
when a shedding flower decides to rest
 on your curly hair and Blue's eyes.
Let's go swim in the lake and drop a seashell in
to wait for us till we come again.
I told you, you don't need
 to choke me to hear your name .
My love for you is a quiet lighthouse.
With no boats to the other shore .

I'm the fixed foot of John Donne's compass.

I will wait for you with our Blue

till you finally come home

and let's go swing on the birches never bent.

Let's be all green and all flowers.

I'm tired of dark and red lipsticks.

Take me to Banaras or the Niles's embrace.

Let's live inside their prayers under the water.

Let's watch death walking on the water , above our heads.

Can you see the screaming souls?

in the riverbank never finding the doors to heaven and earth.

You see, I'm not shivering and still warm.

I told you I'm a quiet lighthouse.

with no boats to other shore

only waiting for you to come home.

Ravi Chettan

I wake up to the mornings in Kerala when Blue
unties my hair and runs with the only hair bun I have.

The rest obviously went missing and I would never
find who hid it. Living with three dogs is a forever
hide and seek game.

I'm always in their game even when I'm sleeping
and having a panic attack. I walk Blue in the backyard
to our favourite Peepal tree near the pond my brother
used to swim before.

There are these tiny birds Blue is fond of. Very tiny
birds.

I keep asking Amma the names of the birds.

She keeps changing the names every day. I call them
sunbirds.

My brother says she is a disgrace to Salim Ali.

I can laugh at his comment because I can afford to be
hard-core politically incorrect here.

Muthu and Ajun wait for their turn impatiently
to walk on the coconut tree lying dead on the ground.
Ammini chechi says last year's storm wiped out a lot of trees.
The storm she had only seen.

I forgot to steal the gate key from my Achan's armoire.
There is Ravi chettan's farmhouse,
we used to go to before.
Amma doesn't allow us to roam around there after
he hangs himself on a Mango tree.
The tree still mourns for his loss
bearing no mangoes thereafter.
The summer saw no mangoes all these years.

We ran back home
 when we saw Ravi chettan calling us
with a handful of ripe and golden mangoes.

Lucid Dreams

A part of me died today /

I was walking back to the scooty I parked at the railway parking lot /

and I knew I'm mourning to your death /

I would recover from your loss only when I leave this place /

It won't be the same /

The distance is going to kill us /

I'm going to torture you /

and you would definitely torture me /

I want to remind myself that I have to pay the price for loving /

Nothing comes free you would say /

Please feel free to judge me with the scale of Sonnets and Septets /

Don't you think I at least want to live a day of Robert Brooke or Walt Whitman /

I would rather be the woman they never loved than be the poets /

The liars of love and truth /

I'm not going to make you my poems /

I'm not going to metaphor my pain and publish a book /

I was smoking when I texted you "I'm going to fuel this pain for something productive" /

I can see where my productivity would lead me /

A part of me wants to go Banaras and smoke flowers /

Have you seen the sky today? /

It was green and purple /

The same color of your t-shirt I'm going to wear every day till it loses your smell /

I stole a lock of your hairs /

and planted it with the rose cuttings in my balcony /

Believe me I only did to write poems and make people go insane /

Believe me you are not my poems /

and I'm not a poet /

Have you ever read a poem 'who' wants to be a novel to live in people's bookshelves and book stores? /

I'm the only poem you would buy and never read /

Hold my hands /

and I would teach you to fall in love with me again /

Please don't take breath /

Close your eyes and jump with me /

There is a garden down the valley where Eve waits for us /

Kiss my lips /

and you will know you are my Adam /

Behind Your Name

Love me when I can't remember my name.
Be my poem.
Give me lilies and make me your garden.
There is a spider in my brain who keeps talking.
Be my poem and die in my heart.
I will plant you somewhere.
Somewhere you can only breathe my tears
and hold my hands .
Hide me in your curls.
Close the door and pray for us.
Let them knock and break the windows.
Let us not hang ourselves in the curtains.
Let us live some more days.
Some more winters and snows.
Let me buy us some more rainbows.
Let it rain and let us not drown.
Wait for me to come in your dreams.

and sing you all my heart and lullabies.
Be my spider and poison me in love.
Keep talking to me.
Keep webbing me till I'm boneless.
I have no eyes and two hearts.
Can you stop me before I cross the sea ?
I'm an island with no trees.
The dessert with blue waves.
Why do I see blue everywhere?
Can't you see I'm going everywhere
but running back to your arms ?
Consume me before I go with the wind again.
Show me your veins and love.
Let me hide in your curls a little longer
till they find me and walk me to my death.
Can I stay a little longer?
Be my ghost and haunt me.
Hide me somewhere they can't find me.
Let them break the doors and scream my name.
Hide me somewhere they can't find me.

Can I stay forever somewhere in you?

Hide me in your veins and paintings.

Hide me somewhere before they catch me

and flash me the sanity.

Let me love you a little longer before I die in their lies.

Tell me you love me.

Scream me your heart

and pour me your blood.

Let me stay a little longer

before they kill you and find me alive to put me in to blue pills.

Flowers of Sunsets

This is not a poem.

This is a nightmare who wants to be a poem.

I always have the burden of making everything into a poem,

So that people won't see how sick I'm.

But I'm so tired of living in all the lies,

The lies that made me sicker than I ever was.

I wish if I could breathe free for once,

To know how it feels all normal and healthy.

I have forgotten how I lived,

All I remember is this suffering.

The pain I can't name,

I tried giving it a lot of names to get away from everything that scares me to death.

It pains me more when I feel how I feel,

It's terrible.

So terrible that I don't mind dying in empty hands, empty promises.

I wake up breathless every morning,

Not knowing to be sad or happy of having survived another night.

I'm not quite sure how I would start the day,

If everything about it could consume me entirely.

Would you believe if I say this is not raw?

I decorated it so much for all of you.

No one can possibly take my rawness,

People always want it with some flowers and sunsets.

I could borrow some for my next poem.

This is nameless.

Not even a poem or muse.

It ends here with an empty scream.

Baptize Empty Tears.

Baptise me with your empty tears again

Let me hold you one more time

I can see us walking onto the sea

I want to warn you

We are not Messiah and Peter

Don't you see where the Strom is taking us

But all you say is" Be of good cheer; it is I; be not afraid "

How funny.

I wish if you just die

Die in my hands before I kiss your curly hair

Oh your hair !!

How I wish to stare you burning

with your books and my hickeys

I just want you die.

Die in my hands

before you choke me to death
when I scream your name.
Die before I love you.
Die before you become a poem
I simply put down to get away with the night.
You see I can live with the sun.
I can eat bacon, black pudding,
and baked beans and tomatoes for breakfast.
Like a normal person who goes to work,
Who goes to college,
who goes to do anything that seems significant,
than breathing the rotten potatoes
you bought and never cooked.

You see I'm not that poet,
Who writes about compass and nightingale,
and make you believe in love.
I'm sorry my poems are the worms,
I can spit and crawl through the nights.
You see I can't sleep,

I sit with the nights and suffer alone.
I can't tell who is more tired,
and who needs whom.
I can tell there are a few
stay burdened with themselves at night.
I want to call them for dinner.
Only to watch them eating the Fish and chips
and laugh at their final seizures and blue lips.
Didn't I warn you my favorite color is blue?

Mermaids

There is no blood in my sin but flowers.
 Teach me to wear them again.
What a misery it would have been
If I could not tell you
there are no more sunsets,
 waiting for you.
No more sky and stars.
Come with me to walk on the shores.
I will show you the mermaids who can't swim.
Give them your tears and
let them swim before
they become the ghost of you,
with no blood in their sin.

Home

I thought I was nowhere.
but I live inside your poems.
I have nowhere else to go.

Funeral

I'm at your funeral before you die.
I see your lies waiting for you to die,
waiting for you to close your eyes,
so, they can jump to the sea,
to drown themselves,
scaring to be the ghost of you.
I see people crying,
wearing your guilt in black
wanting to die with you.
I want to warn them you didn't die.
I want them to catch the fire,
they thought you live in,
only to realize its only painted doors,
and you live in the luxury,
of other's pain.

I wish if you stop,
dancing on your coffin
to tell you that death is silent.
I can lend you some silence,
If you stop pretending dead
people can go home,
not wearing your guilt in black
leaving your demons to sit and cry
for the people you never loved.

Palace Of Lies

I sit with you and your lies

Start talking to me in a language you can't lie.

I can find them in the words you carelessly put,

In the corners of your eyes, the smirks you tried to hide.

The hands I kissed and everywhere I touched, and you bloomed.

I can hear your thoughts and hang myself there.

Stop thinking louder, I can hear them, one by one.

I touch you with my trembling hands, knowing I won't breathe truth again.

I bury myself in your lies and in the palaces, you built in people's hearts.

You want me to be queen of the king you never were.

I die every day, selling the stories I never lived.

I woke up to your mornings, knowing I couldn't kill you with my night.

You never die, no matter how I run away from your palace,

I reach at never-ending doors.

All I want is to see some sky and hope the sun will come.

I'm tired of stars and nights and you.

'You' is a tiring word I give rent to people for some love and cigarettes.

I make them play Bonnie and Clyde till you return home,

All hungry for my love and poems.

You kiss me till I forget all my lovers.

I wake up to the morning being your queen again,

And failing to find you in the palace you died a decade ago.

Final Calling

Today I can walk to my own coffin,

and declare I'm dead.

I want everyone who tried to sell their stories,

to come and visit me for the last time.

Try selling it with a handful of truth this time.

I can try eating it without choking myself to death again.

Claustrophobic Memories

That was a time I could pack my bags and go,

To mountains, to snow, to sea, and anywhere people welcomed me.

I was almost like the wind, going and going, and never reaching anywhere.

Then one day, I stopped running.

There were still voices in the head, but I was too tired to run.

Too tired to fear. Too tired to remember.

Now I can look back and take any memory in my hand.

I can fire my hands with them, but I'm sure I won't get burned even if I want.

Fishing Death

I want the seven of us die.
Die when we are asleep.
Die without knowing we are dying.
I don't want anyone left,
to live in our memories.
I hope there is no life after.
Not coming here again
In another name and flesh.
Not another sight of life.
Not here, not anymore.
We have no last words to anyone.
We want the world,
not to remember us.
Memories have a way of
bringing life again.

Another touch of the sun
will kill us again.
No more blood, no more sky.
Let not even quietness know,
how we died in laughter.
We will certainly miss the prank of life.
We baked the luxury of it every day.
Served it equally and
took it with other pills.
This time the world will be amnestic.
No more trials, no more witchery.
One more night and staring spells.
we will die without telling you,
Life is death's nightmar,
you will never wake up from.

Cobwebs

I spent all my day,
searching for the cobwebs
searching for a spider tirelessly
making his home.
I'm learning to spin webs,
hoping to throw over you,
to see you unmoving
and to look at your eyes
unblinking and constant.
I'm sure we fall in love again.
My venom glands making you blue.
Do you still want to call me sky?
Do you feel loved,
When my digestive fluid
making you all juicy?
You were a tombstone,
With no wildflowers blooming

With no soul graved.
The sun is dying.
You will be home soon.
Let me find a spider,
before I die in your love.

Blue Moon

Take me home,
before I eat blue moon
and vomit your name.
Tell me how to breathe again.
Teach me how to walk.
Hold me to your love,
before I fry my fingers
to feed the barking dogs.
Run to me
before I open door.

Take me home,
before they fire my bones
and lullaby me to a ghost.
Take me home,
before they see my fangs.
Take me home,

before they ring the bell.
Take me take me take me home,
before I scream your name
before they undress me
before I bleed you out.
Let me run to the door,
Run, run, run, run
before they grab my hair
and open my legs.
Take me home,
to teach me to walk again.
and let me walk you.
To the love they couldn't touch.

Capsuled Poems

No one buys my trauma,
If it's not my poem.
I can't keep on writing.
I'm tired of words.
I'm tired of emotions.
If only I can prescribe them in capsules
Some tell me I'm funny.
If only I can tell them
I see them hanging on the air
Who doesn't laugh for that?
Yes, I admit there are some days.
I pretend I'm Cathy Carruth,
writing Unclaimed Experience
If only I inhale trauma to my articles
If only it finds home
but it keeps coming back to me,
again, again and again

Like a stray dog I choose not love
I don't want them to know love.
I don't want them to howl all nights,
looking for the lost love in strange roads
Let them die of hunger,
but not by memories.

Egg Toast

No matter how much I poisoned
the egg toast, he is not dying.
He came alive for the dinner.
I let the candle to fire his hair.
I forgot he was a firefly.
My handguns keep missing.
Finally, I found them in the dustbin.
Where did I lose my fingers,
to pull the trigger?
Will you search the knives in the kitchen drawers?
Wait, my house has no doors.
Tell me, how do I burn myself again
before you scatter
my ashes in the Ganges?

About the Author

Remya Ramakrishnan

Remya Ramakrishnan is a writer and a doctoral candidate in English literature at Vellore Institute of Technology, Vellore. She is exceedingly interested in creating writing and excelled in working with words. She is former writer in Ukiyoto and published an anthology of poems, BLUE VEINS in 2022. She also published a book in Malayalam, NEELAJARMBUKal in 2021 and various short stories in Malayalam and English. She was a former article writer at Way2News and currently focuses on her research on War Trauma. She aspires to coin a new theory on Trauma Studies to capsule the parasite of trauma creating emotionally handicapped society.